to all the children who ever feel alone and abandoned

Published by 99 Series, LLC

ISBN13: 978-1941308981

A message from the author

Do you have bad dreams? If you could use your imagination to train your bad dreams, where would you start? Having bad dreams does not mean we can't change them. We can learn to put aside our bad memories and replace them with good ones. Sometimes if we do or think about happy things, the bad feelings can be replaced. Elliott's *How to Train your Dreams* uses the train metaphor as it reflects the real life events of a young boy who struggled with hard days. He learned to go to happy places that helped him feel better.

While most children have happy childhoods, many children will never know one, let alone a good one. *How to Train your Dreams* takes the reader through one week of Elliott's childhood. He shares his story of training his dreams in hopes of encouraging other children who are going through a hard time to share their voices and how they can teach others to overcome their challenges.

Elliott falls asleep at his desk.
He begins to dream about himself as a
boy. Elliott dreams about a train ride.

As his grandfather is walking him home from
school Elliott begins to feel sad.

He makes his grandfather walk slowly as he
knows what will happen when he gets home.

As Elliott gets closer to home he walks past another school. Elliott sees the kids playing together in that schoolyard. He wants to stay and play too but his mom is waiting for him. "I really don't want to go home," mumbles Elliott.
"I never play outside. I have no friends."

As Elliott walks into his house his mother yells, " Elliott, you have to go to the corner store. We need bread and milk." " But it's raining mom!" cries Elliott.

" Take your umbrella and go right now! " Elliott reaches into the closet, takes his favorite white umbrella and leaves.

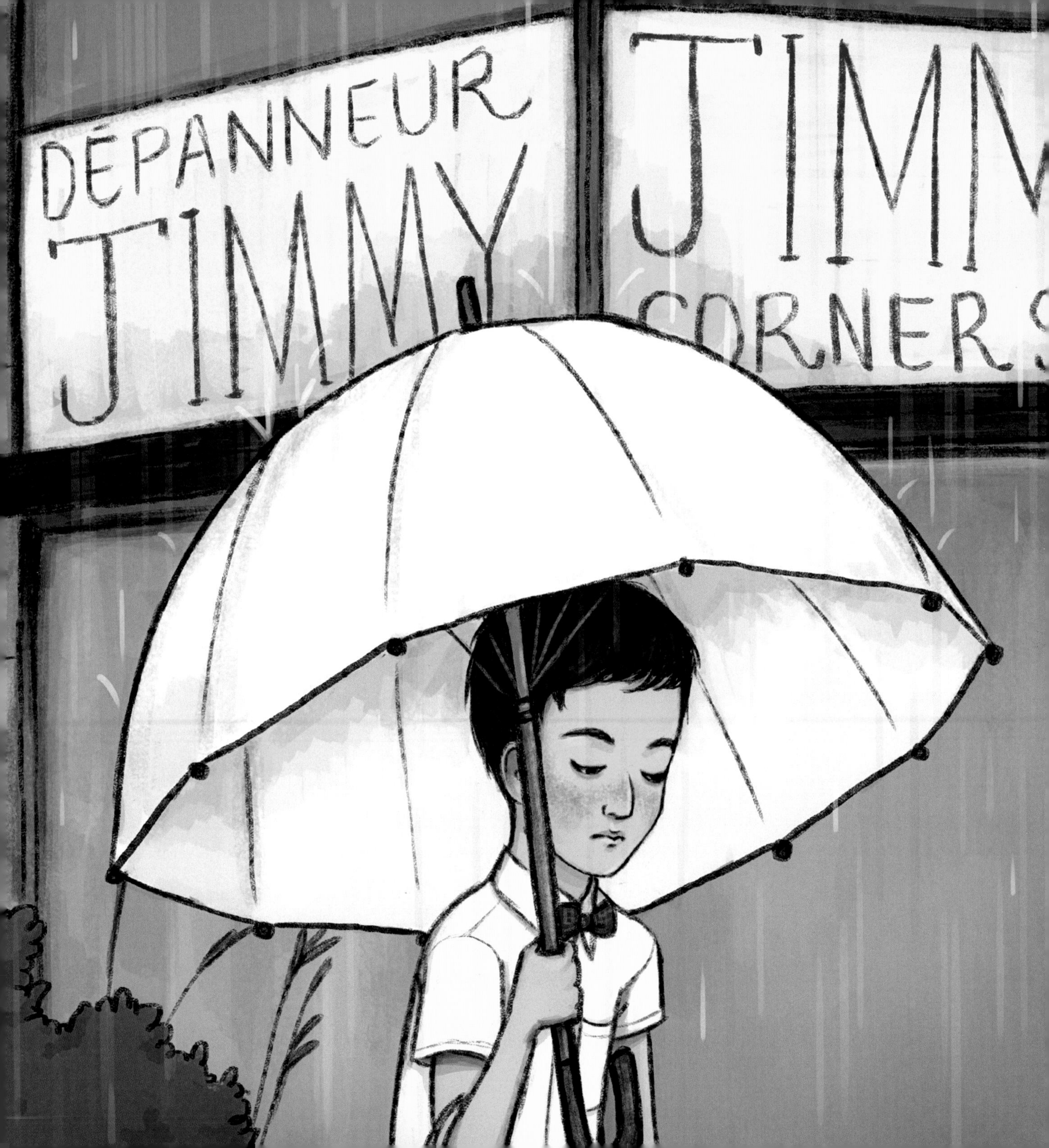
DÉPANNEUR
JIMMY
JIMM
CORNERS

Elliott enters Jimmy's corner store. Jimmy

knows what Elliott needs.

He comes in to buy the same things every week.

As Elliott approaches the counter, he sees

two girls staring at him.

They smile. This makes Elliott shy.

He quickly runs out the door.

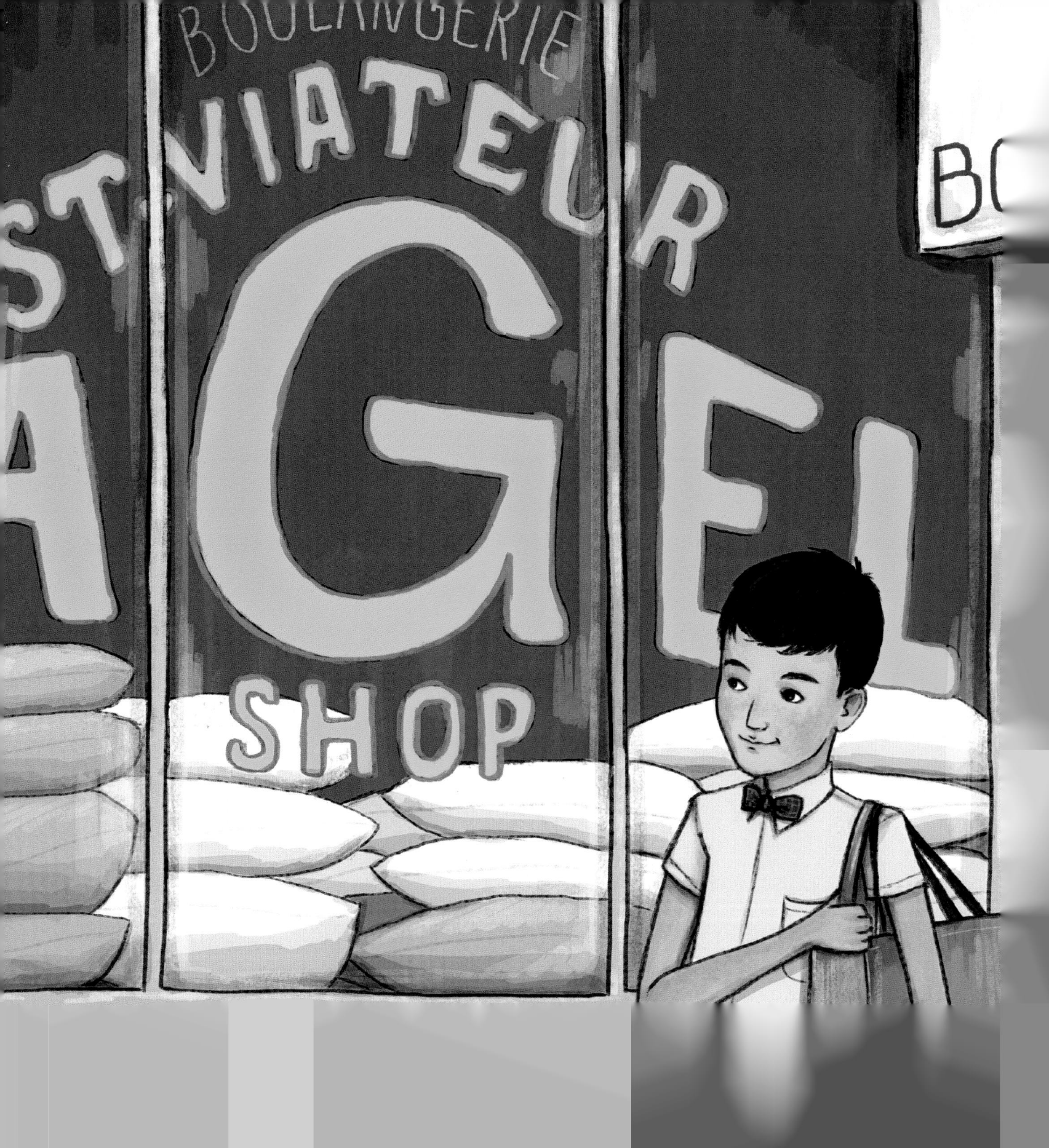
BOULANGERIE
ST. VIATEUR
SHOP

The next day, Elliott repeats one of his errands.

Bagels!

He is so mad at his mom because she always makes

him run errands after school. He can never play

outside. When he gets home from the bagel shop, there is

only time   for dinner, homework and going to bed.

Elliott keeps dreaming. He wants to be happy.
He doesn't like his life. He imagines himself riding on his
red train.
He loves being on his train because he can forget
the bad things that make him sad so he chooses to only
stop at happy places. He imagines himself riding his
bike on a warm and sunny day.

Elliott loves the mountain. He always stares at it from his bedroom window. He imagines riding his bike all around the mountain. Elliott is tired. He stops.

He sits on some steps at the corner of his street to rest. Elliott is almost home.

As Elliott sits on the steps, he feels the sun. It's so warm. Elliott remembers the two people who helped him learn how to make his dreams happy, Ari and Mr. K.

Ari is Elliott's neighbor.
He lives next door.
They are the same age.
Ari and Elliott sit outside on
their balconies and make up
happy stories because they are
not allowed to play downstairs
like the other kids.
The only place he can escape to
is his favorite lane.

Elliott runs into his lane. It's the only place where Elliott can hide from his mom.
He hates his life.
He also hates having bad dreams about it.
He remembers his red train.
He's on it.
He wants his red train to only stop at happy places

As Elliott leaves the lane, he remembers his
last bad dream.

Every Saturday Elliott goes with his mom to
her favorite coffee shop.

He feels that he can never change her and
what she makes him do.

He knows that he can train his dreams however.

He can have happy dreams. Elliott feels excited.

He wants to share his feelings with Mr. K who
owns the bakery shop down the street.

Mr. K is kind to Elliott. He makes Elliott feel special. Mr. K always gives Elliott an onion roll.

Elliott walks by Mr. K's shop on his way home from his last errand. Elliott wants to share something special with Mr. K.

"Mr. K! Mr. K! Guess what?" shouts out Elliott. "I know what to do! I know how to train my dreams! I only make the train stop at happy places".

Elliott was so happy!

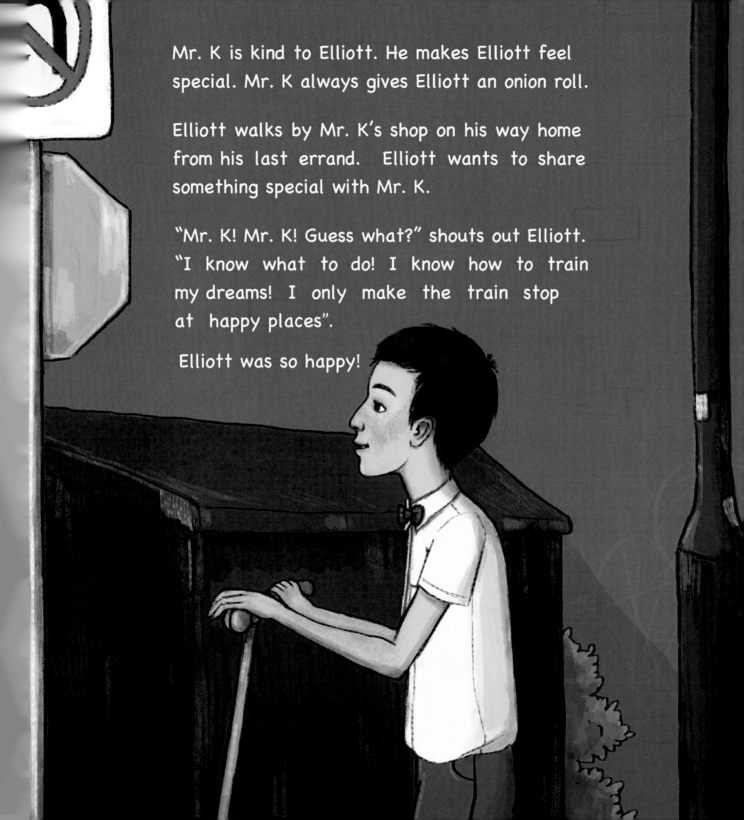

Finally, Elliott wakes up from his nap.

His train ride has come to an end.

He's hungry.

It's time to eat.

Elliott leaves his office and runs across the street to his favorite restaurant, Schwartz's.

He picks up a smoked meat sandwich and a few dill pickles.
It's his favorite errand because it's an errand he does just for himself.

You can help your sad and angry feelings go away by thinking and doing things that only make you happy.

Maria F. Guzzo- *Philanthropist, Author*

Maria F. Guzzo decided to write a children's book *How to Train your Dreams* as her interest in child mental health evolved through her philanthropy. Her shift towards child mental health began in the last few years when she became aware of the *Kids Write Network (KWN)*. Maria decided to adopt the 5-step concept as she was completing her manuscript to better understand how it works. Maria's involvement in her philanthropy is 100% hands-on. Her goal is to help raise awareness of child mental health issues in hopes of reducing the stigma and giving children a fighting chance for a better future.

This September 2015, the Guzzo family's annual charity event in Montreal, the *Notte in Bianco*, will benefit child mental health. Maria has chosen to work and support the *Kids Write Network (KWN)*, a child mental health charity that has developed a 5-step process which helps children work through challenges by using their voices in this new literary and therapeutic method of treatment as they write children's books sharing their experiences and moral lessons. They have created a new imprint of books aptly titled, *Kids 4 Kids*.

Maria has a passion for photography, enjoys travelling and has an appreciation for music from the 60's and 70's. She is currently working on her 2nd book in the child mental health field.

Maria lives in Terrebonne, Québec, Canada with her husband and 5 children.

Paule Trudel-Bellemare- *Illustrator*

Paule Trudel-Bellemare was born in Trois-Rivières Québec, Canada. She studied in Montreal and graduated with a degree in Traditional Animation. She furthered her studies in Fashion Illustration at the Fashion Institute of Technology in New York. Paule free-lances as a fashion and a children's books illustrator.

She lives with her husband, their daughter and a little black pug in a mid-century bungalow of the North Shore suburbs of Montreal.